# Dolphin Dreaming

Story by Jan Weeks
Illustrations by Meredith Thomas

NELSON
A Cengage Company

**Dolphin Dreaming**

Text: Jan Weeks
Illustrations: Meredith Thomas
Editor: Cameron Macintosh
Design: Leigh Ashforth
Reprint: Siew Han Ong

**PM Extras Chapter Books**
**Emerald Level 25-26 Set A**
Dolphin Dreaming
Fish for Dinner
Grand Street Theatre Robbery
Lucky Thursday
Midnight in the Tunnel
Trash and Treasure

Text © 2004 Cengage Learning Australia Pty Limited
Illustrations © 2004 Cengage Learning Australia Pty Limited

ISBN 978 0 17 011430 1
ISBN 978 0 17 011427 1 (set)

**Cengage Learning Australia**
Level 7, 80 Dorcas Street
South Melbourne, Victoria Australia 3205
Phone: 1300 790 853

**Cengage Learning New Zealand**
Unit 4B Rosedale Office Park
331 Rosedale Road, Albany, North Shore NZ 0632
Phone: 0508 635 766

For learning solutions, visit **cengage.com.au**

Printed in China by 1010 Printing International Ltd
23 22

# Contents

# CHAPTER 1

# Mermaid Point

When Dad had to go overseas, he asked my grandparents if Jess and I could stay with them. Mum died when I was a baby and Dad's job takes him away a lot. We spend lots of time with Grandma and Grandpa Ellis. Dad often asks them to look after us. It's an easy solution to the 'what to do with the girls' problem.

Not that we're ever any trouble. We love staying with our grandparents and they like having us. Mum had been their only child, and we're the only family they have left.

This time our stay was going to be different. Grandma and Grandpa Ellis had decided to rent a house for the summer in a little village down the south coast. It was called Mermaid Point. Jess and I had never been there but even its name stirred our imaginations. Our heads were filled with pictures of white sand, sparkling blue water and ships passing by, far out to sea.

"It's going to be so much fun, Tegan," Jess said as she hugged me. "We'll be able to go swimming every day. And we'll get to ride the bodyboards Dad bought us as a going away present. Won't that be fantastic?"

"Great," I answered, not sure I was feeling quite so confident. Jess is two years older than me and she isn't afraid of anything. Jess was born deaf and needs to wear a hearing aid. I was doing my best to be brave like her, but it wasn't easy pretending to be brave when I knew I wasn't. Just about everything scared me.

There was a railway station in a town not far from Mermaid Point. Grandma and Grandpa Ellis had arranged to meet us there. They had come down the week before. It was the first time Jess and I had travelled such a long way by train and we loved it. It made us feel grown up to know that Dad trusted us enough to let us make the trip by ourselves.

As we drew near the station, I began to wonder if it had been such a good idea. "What are we going to do if they are not there to meet us, Jess?" I asked. "What will we do then?"

"You have to stop worrying about everything, Tegan," Jess answered. "They'll be there."

And Jess was right. As the train pulled in, I could see Grandma and Grandpa Ellis standing on the platform, waving to us.

"I told you there was no need to worry," Jess said.

# CHAPTER 2

# The Ledge

The house my grandparents had rented was on a hill. From the front deck, we could look out over the ocean and see the huge rocks that huddled together to form Mermaid Point. Grandpa told us it was dangerous to climb too near the point. He'd heard tales of fishermen who had slipped and fallen to their deaths, especially when the tide was high.

The rocky outcrop separated two beaches. We swam at the one in front of my grandparents' house. To get to the other, we had to climb up the rocks to the path that led along a ledge and down to the rocks on the other side.

We had only been at Mermaid Point two days when Jess said she wanted to explore the second beach.

"It'll be fun," she said, grabbing my arm. "How will we know what's there unless we go and see for ourselves?"

As I looked at the ledge, I wondered if I really wanted to know. The ledge was high and it didn't look very wide. "Why don't we go for a swim instead and leave the exploring for another day?" I suggested.

"We've already been in the water heaps of times," Jess answered. "Come on, Tegan! It isn't dangerous. People walk along the ledge all the time. Why else would there be a path?"

Without waiting for an answer, Jess ran ahead, looking like a mountain goat as she scampered over the rocks. I followed, using my hands to steady myself as I moved gingerly from rock to rock. But getting to the ledge was the easy part.

"I told you it would be fun," Jess said.

The wind was whipping her hair and she laughed as she held out her hand to help me onto the ledge. The path was over a metre wide and cut into the side of a cliff. Tree roots, moss and patches of grass bordered the edge closest to the cliff. On the other side of the path there was a sheer drop.

"Try not to look down," Jess said.

She was too late. I had already done that. Far below me I could see the waves splashing against the jagged rocks, covering everything in white swirling foam. It made my stomach lurch and I felt dizzy. I stood like a statue, frozen with fear.

"Don't be such a scaredy cat, Tegan!" Jess said. She was already half way across the ledge. "Come on! You won't fall."

"I can't," I answered, as I pushed my back into the side of the cliff. "I'm going back."

"Suit yourself," Jess said, as she shrugged her shoulders. "You're the one who is going to miss out. Not me!"

I didn't care. I only knew I had to get off the ledge before I fell off it.

# CHAPTER 3

# The Other Side

I waited on the beach for Jess. She was gone a long time. When she did come back, she couldn't stop talking about the bay on the other side of Mermaid Point.

"You'll never guess what I saw while I was over there," she said. "There was a mother dolphin and her baby swimming in the water. You should have come with me, Tegan. You would have loved them."

Dolphins are my favourite animals. Dad took us to a theme park last year and we saw them doing tricks. I thought then how wonderful it would be to swim with them.

The mother and baby playing in the water on the other side of Mermaid Point were almost enough to make me wish I had gone with Jess. But when I thought of how afraid I'd been on the ledge, I shivered and quickly changed my mind.

Mr Gray was at our house when we got home. He was an old friend of Grandpa's and had moved to Mermaid Point to live after he'd retired. Mr Gray had been the one who suggested my grandparents rent the house.

When Jess told Mr Gray she'd seen dolphins in the bay, he answered that he'd seen them that morning as well. Mr Gray loved fishing and had gone there to throw in his line.

"I think I counted eight of them this morning," he said.

"I only saw a mother and a baby when I was there," Jess answered. "The rest must have swum back out to sea."

"Isn't it dangerous walking along the ledge?" Grandma asked. She didn't want anything to happen to us, especially when she was looking after us.

"Fishermen use the path all the time," Mr Gray answered. "The girls will be safe enough, as long as they keep away from the edge."

"Jess and Tegan aren't likely to do anything silly," Grandpa assured Grandma. He thinks we're both very responsible for our age.

"You're right, of course," Grandma answered, as she smiled at me.

I'm not the one she should be worrying about, I thought. Jess is the daredevil of the family.

"I can hardly wait to see the dolphins again," Jess said that night, as we were getting ready for bed. "We'll go tomorrow morning after breakfast."

"Is there any other way to get there?" I asked, thinking of the ledge and the rocks below it.

"Only if you're a seagull," Jess laughed. "There's no need for you to be frightened, Tegan. You won't fall. I'll help you."

# CHAPTER 4

# Dolphins

That night I dreamt I was swimming with the dolphins. I held out my hand to touch them as they swam around me, playing with me, butting my body with their funny noses, doing acrobatics in the water. It was like I was in a different world, a world so amazing I didn't want to wake up.

When I did, I knew I had to go to the bay to see them. Nobody knew how long the mother and her baby would be there. They could be gone already and I would have missed my opportunity.

The first thing I heard as I sat up in bed was Jess sneezing. Then she began to cough. "We'll have to put off going to the bay for another day," she said. "My head hurts and I feel really sick. I think I'm getting a cold."

My grandparents thought so too and suggested she stay in bed. Jess didn't argue, so I told Grandma and Grandpa that I was going to the beach by myself.

I sat drawing the shape of a dolphin in the sand with a stick and thought about crossing the ledge on my own. If a fisherman had come along, perhaps I might have mustered the courage to tag along behind him. But no fisherman came.

Finally I made up my mind. If I wanted to see the dolphins, I was going to have to cross the ledge by myself.

Once again, climbing the rocks was the easy part. Walking along the ledge was a different story.

"Don't look down," I told myself. "Look straight ahead. Pretend you're walking in the park." It was easy to say, but much harder to do.

Step by nervous step, I inched my way across the ledge until at last I was on the other side.

"There now!" I said to myself. "That wasn't so bad, was it?" But I was already dreading the thought of going back.

The dolphins were still there. Only now there were eight of them. Mr Gray's dolphins had come back. They were swimming in pairs, leaping in the air, then plunging back into the water, only to resurface a few moments later. One had a fish in its mouth. It was tossing it into the air, playing with it. Another swam almost to the beach, before diving under the waves and swimming out into the bay again.

I was so absorbed in their play, I forgot about the ledge. All I could think of was the dolphins. I longed to jump into the water to swim with them, as I had in my dream, but I'm not a strong swimmer, and I thought I might drown. So I sat on a rock, content just to watch them.

# CHAPTER 5

# I Did It!

Before I knew it, hours had gone by. The sun was more than halfway across the sky. It was past lunchtime. Grandma and Grandpa would be wondering where I was.

"I'd better hurry," I told myself as I began to climb up to the ledge.

The wind had blown up and I could hear the waves splashing onto the rocks. I could see them below me, waiting for me to fall.

"I can't do it!" I yelled as I pushed my back into the cliff. "I'm too scared!"

Nobody heard me, except for some gulls flying overhead, and they didn't care whether I fell or not. "Don't be such a baby!" I told myself. "You have to go back. Grandma and Grandpa will be worried about you."

With my back pressed against the cliff and my heart pounding, I took a small step sideways.

Realising I wasn't going to fall, I took another step and then another, until at last I reached the rocks on the other side of the ledge. Then all I had to do was climb down to the sand.

Grandma and Grandpa were waiting for me on the beach. They looked pleased to see me. "Jess said you'd be too scared to walk across the ledge," they told me.

"I was scared," I answered. "But I had to see the dolphins before they swam back out to sea."

Jess was sitting in the kitchen when we went back to the house.

"It was brave of you to walk along the ledge on your own," she said. "I'm proud of you, Tegan. You didn't let your fears stop you from doing something that you really wanted to do."

"It was the dolphins that made me brave," I answered. "Without them, I would never have found the courage. Do you want to know something else, Jess? They were worth every minute of it. They were amazing!"